OHIO

Julie Murray

VISIT US AT
www.abdopublishing.com

Published by ABDO Publishing Company, PO Box 398166, Minneapolis, MN 55439.

Printed in the United States of America, North Mankato, Minnesota.
052012
092012

♻ PRINTED ON RECYCLED PAPER

Coordinating Series Editor: Rochelle Baltzer
Editor: Sarah Tieck
Contributing Editors: Megan M. Gunderson, BreAnn Rumsch, Marcia Zappa
Graphic Design: Adam Craven
Cover Photograph: *iStockphoto*: ©iStockphoto.com/Davel5957.
Interior Photographs/Illustrations: *AP Photo*: AP Photo (pp. 21, 23, 25), Larry Crowe (p. 26), Tony Dejak (p. 27), Hans von Nodle (p. 21), The Morning Journal, Paul M. Walsh (p. 26); *Getty Images*: Focus on Sport (p. 21); *Glow Images*: Aflo Relax (p. 30), Superstock (p. 13), Visions of America, LLC (p. 27); *iStockphoto*: ©iStockphoto.com/benkrut (p. 11), ©iStockphoto.com/Davel5957 (p. 9), ©iStockphoto.com/MisterClips (p. 19), ©iStockphoto.com/Mshake (p. 5), ©iStockphoto.com/saffiresblue (p. 17); *Photo Researchers, Inc.*: Ted Kinsman (p. 30); *Shutterstock*: Rudy Balasko (p. 11), Steve Byland (p. 30), Robert J. Daveant (p. 27), Cynthia Kidwell (p. 9), Philip Lange (p. 30), Doug Lemke (p. 29).

All population figures taken from the 2010 US census.

Library of Congress Cataloging-in-Publication Data

Murray, Julie, 1969-
  Ohio / Julie Murray.
    p. cm. -- (Explore the United States)
  ISBN 978-1-61783-373-1
  1. Ohio--Juvenile literature. I. Title.
  F491.3.M872 2013
  977.1--dc23
                          2012015705

Contents

One Nation

The United States is a **diverse** country. It has farmland, cities, coasts, and mountains. Its people come from many different backgrounds. And, its history covers more than 200 years.

Today the country includes 50 states. Ohio is one of these states. Let's learn more about Ohio and its story!

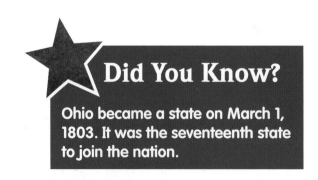

Did You Know?

Ohio became a state on March 1, 1803. It was the seventeenth state to join the nation.

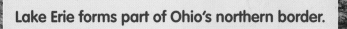

Lake Erie forms part of Ohio's northern border.

5

Ohio Up Close

Did You Know?

Washington DC is the US capital city. Puerto Rico is a US commonwealth. This means it is governed by its own people.

The United States has four main **regions**. Ohio is in the Midwest.

Ohio has five states on its borders. Michigan is north. Pennsylvania is east and West Virginia is southeast. Kentucky is southwest and Indiana is west.

Ohio has a total area of 44,825 square miles (116,096 sq km). About 11.5 million people live there.

REGIONS OF THE UNITED STATES

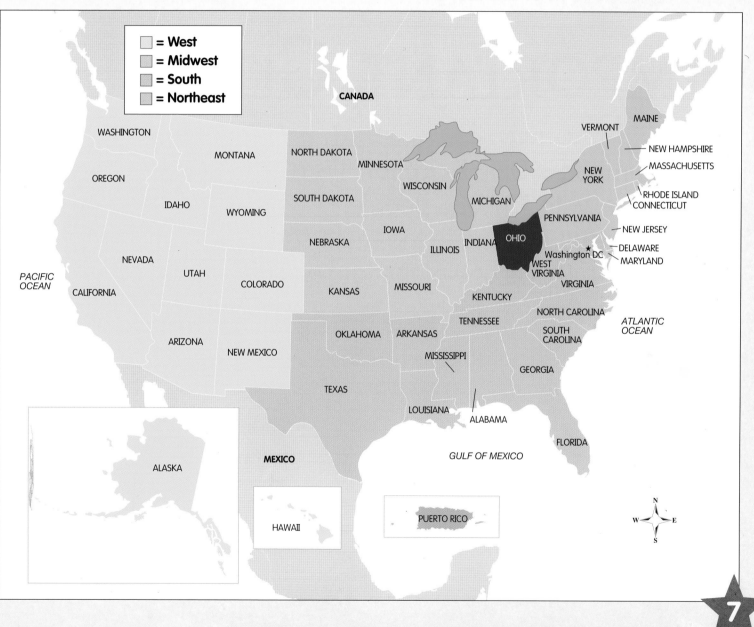

Legend:
- = West
- = Midwest
- = South
- = Northeast

CANADA

WASHINGTON
OREGON
IDAHO
MONTANA
NORTH DAKOTA
MINNESOTA
WISCONSIN
SOUTH DAKOTA
WYOMING
MICHIGAN
NEW YORK
VERMONT
MAINE
NEW HAMPSHIRE
MASSACHUSETTS
RHODE ISLAND
CONNECTICUT
PENNSYLVANIA
NEW JERSEY
IOWA
NEBRASKA
ILLINOIS
INDIANA
OHIO
DELAWARE
Washington DC
MARYLAND
NEVADA
UTAH
COLORADO
KANSAS
MISSOURI
WEST VIRGINIA
VIRGINIA
KENTUCKY
CALIFORNIA
PACIFIC OCEAN
ARIZONA
NEW MEXICO
OKLAHOMA
ARKANSAS
TENNESSEE
NORTH CAROLINA
SOUTH CAROLINA
ATLANTIC OCEAN
MISSISSIPPI
GEORGIA
TEXAS
LOUISIANA
ALABAMA
FLORIDA
GULF OF MEXICO

ALASKA
MEXICO
HAWAII
PUERTO RICO

N
W E
S

IMPORTANT CITIES

Columbus is Ohio's **capital**. It is also the largest city in the state, with 787,033 people.

Columbus is home to the main campus of Ohio State University. This is one of the largest US colleges.

Ohio

Cleveland

★ Columbus

Cincinnati

The Ohio Statehouse is more than 150 years old. Up close, visitors can see fossils in the limestone it was built from.

The Scioto (seye-OH-tuh) River flows through Columbus.

Cleveland is Ohio's second-largest city. It is home to 396,815 people. Cleveland is a **transportation** center for the Midwest. It has an important port. It is on Lake Erie and at the mouth of the Cuyahoga River.

Cincinnati (sihn-suh-NA-tee) is the third-largest city in the state. It has 296,943 people. Mount Airy Forest is one of the city's many parks.

Cleveland is home to the Rock and Roll Hall of Fame and Museum.

Cincinnati is on the Ohio River.

11

OHIO IN HISTORY

Ohio's history includes Native Americans and settlers. The Adena and Hopewell were two Native American tribes in the area. They were known for making dirt mounds. They used these for burials and **ceremonies**.

Around 1670, French explorers claimed land in present-day Ohio. In 1763, England gained control of this land. In 1787, it became the Northwest Territory. The area's first **permanent** settlement was formed the following year. Then in 1803, Ohio became a state.

Serpent Mound was built by the Adena. It looks like a giant snake. It is in southwestern Ohio.

Timeline

1825

The Erie Canal was completed. This important waterway connects the Atlantic Ocean with the Great Lakes.

1869

The Cincinnati Red Stockings became the first **professional** US baseball team.

1803

Ohio became a state on March 1.

1800s

An important battle was fought on Lake Erie during the **War of 1812**. After the war ended in 1815, thousands of settlers moved to Ohio.

Thomas Edison of Milan invented the lightbulb.

1879

1813

1913

Heavy rain caused the worst flooding in Ohio's history. About 350 people died and many buildings were ruined.

1967

Carl Stokes became mayor of Cleveland. He was the first African-American leader of a major US city.

2010

LeBron James of Akron left the Cleveland Cavaliers basketball team after seven years. He joined the Miami Heat.

1900s

2000s

The first electric traffic lights were set up in Cleveland. James Hoge invented them.

1914

Astronaut Neil Armstrong of Wapakoneta became the first man to walk on the moon.

1969

ACROSS THE LAND

Ohio has hills, forests, and cliffs. It also has a lot of waterways. The Ohio River forms the state's southern and southeastern borders. Lake Erie forms part of the northern border.

Many types of animals make their homes in Ohio. These include white-tailed deer, woodchucks, wild turkeys, and walleyes.

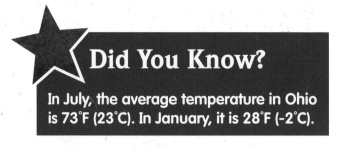

Did You Know?

In July, the average temperature in Ohio is 73°F (23°C). In January, it is 28°F (-2°C).

The Hocking Hills area is known for its beautiful waterfalls.

EARNING A LIVING

Ohio has important businesses. Most people work in service jobs, such as selling goods, buildings, or land. This state is also known for manufacturing many products. These include machinery, metals, foods, soap, and tires.

Ohio has many natural **resources**. Its mines produce coal and natural gas. And, the state has rich soil for farming.

Corn (*above*) and soybeans are Ohio's most important crops.

Sports Page

Many people think of sports when they think of Ohio. It has been home to famous athletes over the years. The state also has well-known **professional** football, basketball, and baseball teams.

College football and basketball are popular sports in Ohio. Many people watch Ohio State University football games. They are played in Columbus at Ohio Stadium, which is called "the Horseshoe."

Pete Rose of Cincinnati was a famous baseball player. He helped the Cincinnati Reds win two World Series.

Jesse Owens was a popular runner who grew up in Cleveland. He won four Olympic gold medals in 1936.

Jack Nicklaus is considered one of the best golfers of all time. He is from Columbus.

HOMETOWN HEROES

Many famous people are from Ohio. Ulysses S. Grant was born in Point Pleasant in 1822. He led the Northern troops during the **American Civil War**.

In 1869, Grant became the eighteenth US president. He served until 1877. He helped the United States rebuild after the war.

Did You Know?

Ohio is sometimes called "the Mother of Presidents." That's because seven US presidents have been born in this state!

Grant's given name was Hiram Ulysses Grant.

23

Neil Armstrong was born in Wapakoneta in 1930. He is a famous **astronaut**.

On July 20, 1969, Armstrong became the first person to walk on the moon. He is known for saying, "That's one small step for man, one giant leap for mankind."

★★★★★★★★★★★★★★★★★★★★★★★★★★★★★★★★★★

Armstrong (*center*) traveled with Buzz Aldrin (*left*) and Michael Collins (*right*) in the Apollo 11.

Tour Book

Do you want to go to Ohio? If you visit the state, here are some places to go and things to do!

★ Taste

Try some Cincinnati chili. This type of chili features unusual spices such as cinnamon or chocolate. It is served over spaghetti or hot dogs, sometimes with cheese or other toppings.

★ Play

Ride a roller coaster at Cedar Point in Sandusky. This famous amusement park has more than 16 of them! It is located on the shores of Lake Erie.

★ Cheer

Watch the All-American Soap Box Derby. This car race has been held in Akron since 1935. It features kids who have made their own race cars.

★ Discover

Check out the Rock and Roll Hall of Fame and Museum in Cleveland. There, you can learn about many famous musicians.

★ Remember

Learn about the nineteenth US president at the Rutherford B. Hayes Presidential Center in Fremont. He was one of the seven presidents born in the state.

A GREAT STATE

The story of Ohio is important to the United States. The people and places that make up this state offer something special to the country. Together with all the states, Ohio helps make the United States great.

Ohio is known for its forests. It is called "the
Buckeye State" because of its buckeye trees.

Fast Facts

Date of Statehood:
March 1, 1803

Population (rank):
11,536,504
(7th most-populated state)

Total Area (rank):
44,825 square miles
(34th largest state)

Motto:
"With God, All Things Are Possible"

Nickname:
Buckeye State

State Capital:
Columbus

Flag:

Flower: Scarlet Carnation

Postal Abbreviation:
OH

Tree: Ohio Buckeye

Bird: Northern Cardinal

Important Words

American Civil War the war between the Northern and Southern states from 1861 to 1865.
astronaut a person who is trained for space travel.
capital a city where government leaders meet.
ceremony a formal event on a special occasion.
diverse made up of things that are different from each other.
permanent lasting or meant to last.
professional (pruh-FEHSH-nuhl) working for money rather than for pleasure.
region a large part of a country that is different from other parts.
resource a supply of something useful or valued.
transportation the act of moving people or things from one place to another.
War of 1812 a war between the United States and England from 1812 to 1815.

Web Sites

To learn more about Ohio, visit ABDO Publishing Company online. Web sites about Ohio are featured on our Book Links page. These links are routinely monitored and updated to provide the most current information available.

www.abdopublishing.com

Index